CONSCIOUS

MW01382213

to shape

consciousness

ethically

laketime
holding earth, take into account

coffee
water

mug
lake

human
elephant

~

mouths lip

the vase houses

the trunk

the couch

#comedicmaterialism

~

every vessel

is a cave

in time

an e-motion

- in the very infinity that it does propel.

~

to shape

is to give to laketime

the cash money

~

cats dig mugs

~

the vase has a plant in it

~

dawson college's newpaper the plant
which i did write for and did edit #unemployabledudechilling

~

mug touches the human to the animal
to the lake tothe swirls
earth

in the galzazxises of infinite racist hate

~

"i love evil" (frank o'hara)

- #comedicmaterialism

~

"and what you laugh at will be hip anyway" (amiri baraka)

#comedicmaterialism

~

~ so the coin

is reiterated -

the raven
notes
the rasp

sunchokes -

as the numbers house the values e-designated by God. #comedicmaterialism

I'M IN IT

~

"This is a black day for B.C. Parks –"

~

the provincial government
is ensuring that none of our parks are now safe from industrial development," she said.

revaluing the animals, unknown
the animals

thoughts
e-animation

of the animals
in the chemicals

in the physical minds of the humanities

as these cats revalue the real

being onto the spiritual

in our phono=textual

being together
as

langu[/ages]
so

the spiritual is out of sight
pacific /never again

species especial/ocean

of the void / as e-cpomutations

~

- so the quantum-typo

flow
bleeds all squiggly

in the Body, as night-time

take back power

in the sublation

of the father
inside the mother

of infinity

-or something, my sweet.

~

what is a
park

~

in which bills misunderstand
as one

so another

This Bill undermines the very definition of what a 'park' is,

my love

~

displaced
upon the wilderness of the spiritual

disgraced
standing under the very

definitely
placing protected activities industrial / upon the real

~

as i sit as alien
watching my powers displaced

so the #yeezus
of the west

finds its value
as the reign of alien light, so the right

comes into force on the date
of Royal Assent.

as the hermeneutic of suspicion
does annex the stars

e-coins
dendrofactify

in an e-phallotransmutation
into the dual
~

orchid of e-phallocomputation.
the swantological superposition,

the stars do return
to these humanities

- so the e-sexe

is undervalued.

~

- so the numbers

house
the values|

e-designated
by god. so what?

~
dendrofactifying
belief,

critical faith

that real eSOIL/facticity

~

should i had been a pear-

so
poetic composition,

a technique of improvisation/
activation

being with you
always already intentionally being with you

as desires,

eating the facticity in our fucking moments into its really-desired reality,

~

in the ideal between earth and space
and our neuropsychotransmutational e-production

of the animals(chemical)
of infinite re e-valuation - e-coins
of those private spheres of human animality, the breasts of women

- of the seafloor -
to the flower

of the demonic ,

of authenticity, my stars

laketime
oppose
to numbs

~

as the hermeneutic of suspicion
does annex the stars

e-coins
dendrofactify

in an e-phallotransmutation
into the dual
~

orchid of e-phallocomputation.
the swantological superposition,

the stars do return
to these humanities

~

- so
the coin
is uttered.

+

~

sell
to earth -

renovate?

our co-rectitude

- in the clouds, my sweet.

- so
the soil
is factified.

~

the word
turns

Saint
Moncton

on

~

to the

material #comedicmaterialism
supposed!

~

in faith

- as the crocodile
of the ideal

- alas.

as fredricton the entertainer

~

its monetary
tear

upon the water

~

- so does my poetry
oppress.

/

and venues -

these do not

suppose
the matter /

~

as decay

as it inheres if the sleep

is remembered

in the images

of human -produces. eating

~

the number
as animals

as Spoons
as Blurs

of the ripples of antecedent /
laketime

~

NOT SO MANY WATER

COLOUR AS NUMBER O MY JESUS FUCK
CHRIST

~

-= so does
the grape
pulp taste

as the water
its sweet
cunning

- as venues in our shelves.

~

in which the marijuana /

usually is stored

~

at what cost? the alternative

intention/illeity

as it is in stars /

animals all

/ each taste

taste as for paws
- and fangs. /

~

and also the sex organs, facts of the chemical(soul) in our astral "being" with "you"

(Fan Wu , "upon the supposition

of a swantology
of laketime / as being itself

/the two-step
critically

towards
an ethics of fun"

57 - 96j) - so the verse

confounds the lake
of basis ~

in which everyone

~

does bodily take power / in a

aquarium

whom the surreal (lake

does underwrite (ontario

~

of our secret

value,
my love

~

as e-Halifax does radiate talent, so the alien e-produces e-Halifax
- or does it e-xplode?

~

~

, girl. #howtodothangswithwords

~

~

in the conflict of the atmo-sp
heres

ofcreature-production, the brahman

of the real
is

as art displaced
in its own

facticity

~

so that the jewels
asleep

on the neck

-lace of the press
does replace
the ab

-sence of a

trace
exact

of Calgary"

-- Christ

Inject dye into the bloodstream for x-rays

Make corrections on copy for books or magazine articles

~

Conduct improvisations to test mathematical theories

~

Print maps of the ocean floor,
Plan a strategy to create a major forest fire

Represent in court.
Work in a green house to crossbreed plants.
Operate in exoerunebtak farms growing flowers.

~

Save trees by trimming dead branches

Write critical reviews

Use advanced math to put people to sleep - then use a camera

to make traggic flow smoothly.

~

#comedicmaterialism

In other words, all human, anthropogenetic desire--the desire that generates self-consciousness, the human reality--is, finally, a function of the desire for "recognition." And the risk of life by which the human reality "comes to light" is a risk for the sake of such a desire. Therefore, to speak of the "origin" of self-consciousness is necessarily to speak of a fight to the death for "recognition."

i

the e-production of desire is not limited to the human reality; the animal
e-produces as well

ii

i placed a mug in the cavity

iii

operate on a company's accounting procedures, rippling the lasso
- locating the most commercially profitable sponges.

iv

tell me, Kojeve -

Without the fight to the death for pure prestige, there would never be the slave who, in binding himself completely with animal life is merely one with the the natural world of things. By refusing to risk his life in a fight for pure prestige, he does not rise above the level of animals. Hence he considers himself as such, and as such is considered by the master. But the slave, for his part, recognizes the master in his human dignity and reality, and the slave behaves accordingly. The master's "certainty" is therefore not purely subjective or "immediate," but objectivized and "mediated" by another, the slave's, recognition.

v

giving it up
for the lasso

numbering the humanities, tagging the humanities

~

vi

all of the matter as we field it zumbiologically does too e-produce - the sun
that blue mug of outer space, does encrypt

its e-mail to the jungle. The jungle
grows in this like

weird dream continuum, and

xii

accepting into the open slip

its e-knowledge of that void
of impossibility

e-materials
of weird space

genuflects, so to speak - it accepts
the superposition

of dendrofactifying rhizomatic e-production - , girl

vii

my poetry is the supreme fiction, woman.

xix

it is so limited
to think of animals

as incapable, of the world of e-production
as it is constricted

by the human contract
my love.

the sun does too send its e-mail
to the tree. the tree

is in communication of
a kind we totally disrespect

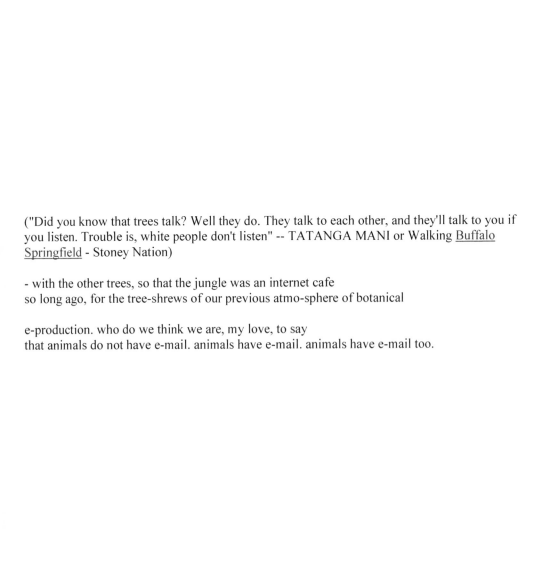

("Did you know that trees talk? Well they do. They talk to each other, and they'll talk to you if you listen. Trouble is, white people don't listen" -- TATANGA MANI or Walking Buffalo Springfield - Stoney Nation)

- with the other trees, so that the jungle was an internet cafe
so long ago, for the tree-shrews of our previous atmo-sphere of botanical

e-production. who do we think we are, my love, to say
that animals do not have e-mail. animals have e-mail. animals have e-mail too.

I just bombed at the open mic.

These philistines

will not understand

my Canadian Poetry. #comedicmaterialism

~

Jesus Christopher Durning
is language. Language
is Jesus Christ. Jesus Christopher Bathgate

is iterated infinitely

in the game |

~

of botanical e-production. Jesus Christyne Mathison is too good.
Jesus Christopher Kung is "to god"

understood infinitely,
infinitely understood.

~

underrated

in the game

~

of botanical e-production. #foraging

~

eating momentum

into facticity

~

as

prayer? / to the earth in itself (the blue rocks? are you hip?

deep inside
inside the earth

~

- but it is what it is,

~

dig. #comedicmaterialism

~

ix

digging in
eating

moments, in
my right

pocket, e-producing from the pouch

- as i remove from my pocket

~

notes

- i dig

~

eating
momentum
digits

of lake
time
- e-producing

~

from the couch

- notes

- as the hand
is lost

to the void
of impossibility reduced
replenished - in its
comparison
as the notes
must all stand / at once / under the momentum

of marsupial wonder - so

~

the poet /digs
digging in /

eating everymoment /
in

producing the notes /
carefully, from the pocket - and e-producing

the pencil crayon curls

~

of smoke shavings

~

and lake/time/lack/space

- electricity
of the libraries i do haunt stoned out of my mind,

of that grave
yard of good
hippy

vibes,
this city - heaving rainstorm clouds

of Van Couver

from cows fording the river? feeling excited? me neither? #death

~

smoke weed? don't mind if

i do, Death. so, in the acceptance

~

of Death, because i could not stand
being on

this UFO/of some kind.- as the decomposition

~

zumbifies
factifying

our fine
recreational

tree-ality #afterlife #now #youguys

~

Practice a piece of music until it can be played flawlessly.

~

Lead a project to help establish a cable Internet connection.

~

Never give up. #comedicmaterialism

~

so the hermeneutic of suspicion
computes, as the hermeneutic

of recreation
e-transmutes - what of it? as evolution

so the void
of impossibility - an indivisible quotient

- and the practice of dialectical improv / comedy poetry activism

as pangea/africa (and the ocean floor
of space

of the hominid psyche? (including plants

#controversy

~

replenishing [the void of impossibility
towards evolution/convolution
of our species-being] towards

nir-vana/u-topia
their paradoxical plenitude? smoking
weed, and being reborn - for do not the weeds

turn the soil, as surreal
as zig zab

as atmosphere phenoumenal, a wunsch/by which/in
chillness [chillheit] - letting in

the typos, as the hand
goes into the pouch

so the marsupials the poacher must not touch
- as in the play

the lines
of the removal
of sequence

in order
directs to the real

brahman/illeity
the intentionality

of the speaker - so
a comedic materialist

e-labour
of EVOL

must cogitate
physically / meditate / mediate

a critical faith

in a beyond ideal ideas as as a poetry / "movement of play
that produces" (Derrida

e-differance is the nonfull, nonsimple o"rigin, it is the structural and differing origin of [illegible

~

satyric -
id est, intellext

and body
(subtext)

~

stones
mouth

over
water

value
position

momentum
laketime

rain
iteration

utterance
current

laketime
e-coin.

e-coin. #comedicmaterialism

~

as a way
the tao

so the dialectic / as the comedic
is iteration

of process. so
the fluidity

of the text/reader
dialectic / as the son reads the moon its e-mail from the son

so the father's desire
for the solar energy / to hold

and reiterate
fluidity

of the iteration
of species-being / for the plants and animals.

~

ix

dendrofactify
the stars at night. council

farmers
to help them meet market demands.

dendrofactify in laketime the sublated originary desire
and desire

of the stars night
no struggle

no improvisiation

no origin

no void of impossibility

no hands

~

as numbered position and momentum
is opposed to the real - does the firelight
combust / in the face
of animal-being? as placement /to displacement/poetry
displaced in its own facticity
poetry - positions, practice, activity.

~

leaf
root
earth
panel;

light?
electricity?

do not call it dark energy

~

i am a god!

in my poetry

~

do not call it dark matter

Walk through a redwood forest to estimate timber e-production.

~

Do colour drawings of cars and boats for a magazine. Do chemical research in a college laboratory.

Work in a greenhouse to crossbreed plants #comedicmaterialism

of process. so
the fluidity

of the text-reader
dialextual relation.

~

no originity

~

no hands

~

no dialextual relation

~

two hands
removing the language of advertising

and putting it back into the poetry

~

removing the language of the churches,

putting the phallos back
into the poetry

~

poetry is
of process

and
two hands.

~

in the future
every one will be Jesus

Christ every fifteen seconds
and nowhere in the

time intervening
and everywhere

in the time
intervening

~

the future
will be televised; the television
will not

~

be subtextually botanically e-productive,
every one poetry infinitely iterable.
every poetry the body

of futurity #comedicmaterialism

~

the poet has two hands - they agree, they do not agree #comedicmaterialism

~

the poet is superstructurally infrastructural #thisismybody

the poet is phenoumenal #thisismyblood.

the poet eats
momentum
into facticity? - in the poetry/philosophy/ practice of improvisational

~

the poet eats
momentum
into facticity - dialectical #comedicmatierilrejlikm

~

in the swantological superposition of #comedicmaterialism,

dendrofactifying from this one
superposition rooted
in swantological laketime; blue

"current
playas in the game of infinity" (Mbaruk) #comedicmaterialism

- are you hip? - to the earth
all of human time - the poet

under
this stands,

night

~

over
and
over
and
over
and - so the poet.

~

the poetry enters
the poetry

the poet enters the poetry

the poetry enters the poet #comedicmaterialism

~

the swantologist
zumbifies

sublates
the imagination

in

~

infrastructural laketime
in the swantological superposition

~ a phoenix ~
map

infinite
spoken
lights #profumo

of earthly laketime
atlas

neblulbulbous shoulders of

~

as the swantological yoga
so the zumbiologinal feng shui #comedicmaterialism

in touch
thought

thought
in touch,

man,

~

woman,

with our own
mineral/plant

matter habitat,
our

ur-phenoumenologically
"hebel"-ian infrastructure,
our knowledge

- a zumbiologinal feng shui

~
of biomes of

~

earth* #comedicmaterialism

~

“Vanity of vanities, saith the Preacher,

vanity of vanities; all is vanity” (KJB 1159). “vanity”
trans.
Hebrew “hebel”

“vapour” or “breath”,

~

*knowledge #comedicmaterialism

~

"the comparison of Ecclesiastes to this meditation by
shows further leaves this during the particle physics era kaleidoscope -"
(Alex Cottreau)

"current
playas in the game of infinity" (our understanding

~

space

~

i

as the psyche
of impossibility - an indivisible quotient

eaten
into facticity

into momentum

into facticity,

- in the practice

of dialectical

improv #comedicmaterialism,

~

- so the space
of space

space

~

space #comedicmaterialism - the nonfull, nonsimple originity
of differences

~

originity #comedicmaterialism - dendrofactually absolute knowledge/innocence infinitely e-transmutable [and e-phallocomputation -compatible]

~

as the biome

- so dark matter.

~

as knowledge

- so the white man's field theory

ii

as the psyche
of impossibility - an indivisible quotient

eaten
into facticity

into momentum

into facticity, /- in the practice / of dialectical improv #comedicmaterialism,

~

- so the hermeneutic
of recreation
its transcendental

ideological state
apparatus - its
biome.

a feng shui
of categories

anaesthetic
of dissensus

~

a mobile,
superpositional

feng shui
~infinitecurv
"monetary

must copy

~

- as in the play

the lines
of the removal
of sequence

in order

- so the hands

~

+/$

And he added: 'you feel the full significance of this myth of outside and inside in alienation, which is founded on these two terms.' (Bachelard "the dialectics of inside and outside")

~

so the "laketime" is "in" the "values" of @poetry -

as "In a lecture given by Jean Hyppolite on the subtle structure of denegation (which is quite different from the simple structure of negation) Hyppolite spoke of 'a myth of outside and inside'. (Bachelard "the dialectics of inside and outside")

?

the hermeneutic

of recreation e-produced

id est the poetry - so

the poem poem

is to god

is to be the death and inter-resurrection of facticity

as the swantologist. #comedicmaterialism

~

the zumbiologinal
swantology/feng shui

+/$

~

the biome.

~

first as to slavery. the slave is a piece of property which is animate, slavery is natural; in every department of the natural universe we find the relation of foregrounds and laketime.

(Aristotle, politics}

~

so laketime

as domestic animality

for the humans

the "protective value", "topophilia" (Bachelard)
is a relation of foregrounds/laketime [+/$]

the biome

the position @poetry
is sublated #comedicmaterialism

in

~

laketime

[$/~] - so "the phenoumenology of earth-poetry" (Luther Luther Vandross) in the age of botanical e-production #comedicmaterialism

~

the laketime home swims in the chemicals
and the sleep-buds in ascension

- as the cookie

so the sweet #comedicmaterialism

~

death
of the clouds

+ drops
/

- so

the poet - $

~

as the zumbiologinal
swantology/feng shui

+/$

~

so the hermeneutic

of recreation e-produced

id est the poetry - so

the poem poem

is to god

is to be the death and inter-resurrection of facticity

as the swantologist.

~

the poet

loquor

- so the speaker is $

and the positional @poetry
dislocated

upon the +

~

gently

~

as a practice/philosophy/poetics

- |e-production being natural to us -as also the sense of e-harmony and e-rhythm , the metres being obviously species of humans - it was through our originary play, and by a series of improvements for the most part gradual on their first efforts, that they created poetry out of their improvisations" (Aristotle, Poetics)

- so #comedicmaterialism

~

i think that the poet can be here of use. #comedicmaterialism

~

the slave, in its
animal

domesticity
digs

forepaws
into

foregrounds

gush
of laketime.

~

the biome is a
atmosphere

phenoumenal
of creature-production. housing

the value. dividing
the values. particling

the waves. so the @poetry
does compute.

#comedicmaterialism

~

~

i think the poetics can be
swantology/feng shui

~

of use
here

Andrew Mbaruk please pay me $32.90 CDN for a cellphone battery for use of this image. i need it so i can keep generating #comedicmaterialism -- Lena Suksi

~

at last! my
multi-platform -performable form of tag #comedicmaterialism is, / being e-produced

~

of these animals #ideas
their identities e-designated

by the phallos
under the robes

of being #comedicmaterialism

~

the light
is the community
in the ceramic zeug in its wavicle-foam-momentum as a communion rhythm in/round

laketide #yesnegation

~

nous

les

planets

of the current university

of the perfumes, per-forms,

of the curved
platforms of

the cosmos
infinite of

quantized
tide

foam #comedicmaterialism
seabed

of leaning Lena #inclination

~

so the garrison
does price

the infinite values of publically housed

foams

shaping / [+/$]
as the sky

trains full occupied
would

on the date
4/20

be - so

the hands
and

feet

upon the one of laketide within the deeper laketide - so the [garrison/public house]
fluctuation #comedicmaterialism

- as a materialist

[swantologist/is]

fluxion

~

is

Lena as

does hold

the out

-hold
of the torontologically -quantized zeug

of laketide partaking of the radiation

autobiographic

(digging the Taylor Ableman sense of the word "autobiograph")
of a deeper laketide

in "superpositional balance" (Kant Chatline) of of
of #comedicmaterialism

the swantologist/is
logic

of laketime

- so the swantologist

brands

what of it / we disclose

~

-metatorontologically #comedicmaterialism
#comedicmaterialistically metatorontological

branding the city otherwise [wazungu-wise]
rebranding the fields

into @poetry, the

walt whiteman
quantizes #comedicmaterialism

the public
full biblically

chronicling

the tidal choreograph
of infinite lake-ly rewrites

in the game #comedicmaterialism

asyntactic

of tidal is

#comedicmaterialism

through and through
the swantologist/is

in/it

in/EVOL

must suppose
the biome
andrew's real
brahmin-illeity
in the game
as the sub-altrui
sublated in s/he
subliminally
iterable

in the game #comedicmaterialism

~

the style she does radiate does rebrand the privatized public the pub,

our zeug,

the mug #comedicmaterialism

~

~

the lyricism romantique
of the ecrivant did wax
#comedicmaterialism
~

commonest the implication. #comedicmaterialism
the date of publication
an extravaganza is the revue
the wolf ikjmnabroad. the moan
sea
of reply|
and demand. #comedicmaterialism
in the second hand
~

the metatheatre
of the biome - could
x
there be a metafiction
so? #comedicmaterialism
~

so the work
s
~

the chemically
e-produced
animals
own
memories, grow
full remembered
in it
animals
dendrofactifying
in the fields
of being
legally
zoned, quantized?
in the futurbiome
as
~

1 ripe California avocado, sliced
3 cups iceberg lettuce, shredded
4 or 5 fresh nectarines

Add to @poetry
laketide
tone colour
line endings
in the real
of the #comedicmaterialist poet
this facebook status is infinitely iterable in the game. #comedicmaterialism
~
so
folksong
of the stars
do not sing to me of white
man
field
theory. let the
Capricornus
~
Pegasus
Cassiopeia
up inside
until the
Gemini
still inside
~
a cat is a cat. it
only
is the pet
in
chemical
e-production
the hands
- it is in one
hand, it is in
the other hand, it
is in both hands
to the real
chemical
animal
tracing the infinite into the wavicle-foam
of e-membered
e-produced
totally e-phallocomputationally fielded

in the spheres of the Higgs gaze on
the bosom
of chemical
animal in our e-phallocomputationally dislocationally superpositional
creature-prudence
don't you come out and play #comedicmaterialism underneath the Higgs robes of being, Trinity Review
#comedicmaterialism
~
as the curve of the LP,
HE
was an arrangement in time the @poetry has mastered
- and the hunt for love
as the swantologists - each such
sad world
of hound
of infinity
over its
loss of itself into the literary terms and literary theory
as the principle #comedicmaterialists were rounded
up
and destroyed by concerned
critics. #comedicmaterialism
~
- so
i know
in this position
as the moment of reproduction of the chemical
as the swantologist
in the round #comedicmaterialism
urges its careful
trace
of the yet-not-quite-actually-really-quantized laketide
wavicle-foam
of the chemical creatures of popular cogitation. #comedicmaterialism
in
to the atmo
sphere
of earthly
like
like
lake ly
~

tide
eating Cassiopeia into
facticity
~
#comedicmaterialism
~
This facebook status update is inginally iterable
in the biome
#comedicmaterialism

[+/$]

the laketidal
process [woods, e.g.] #comedicmaterialism

~

e-designates, publishes
throws the

[in
to the dialectical superposition

as

it is pretty easy, the
e-production

of a revolution, comrades - considere, for one instance always outside of time - until it

no one had believed it would become a world movement,

- so #comedicmaterialism

as the poet cuts his teeth

on the stand up comedy open mic scene ub tge city of 93.7 JRfm - Vancouver's New Country

- smoking "mad herb"
as

the sarcasm
gasp

laughters
in these
"a vigorous treasure" (New York Herbal Turban Coffin Illeity)
evergreens

crows
parrots ~ 1995

Venables Street
Vancouver BC V5L 2H6
thecultch.com / the surface

of a bildungsroman
- lost a index

cards / glass

of the window/bricks
do kick open

tide to
mind

dividing
the buds ~ on

the surface

of the index

on the surface

of the zig / zab

publication / privatization
of the real
dialectic, #comedicmaterialism

my comrades
in the paper-trace

~

is infinitely intimated
in the game.

~

am
to "god" #comedicmaterialism

~

as

~

smoke weed every day #comedicmaterialism

~

- do not smoke weed every day - #comedicmaterialism

~

- so the poet "writes" #comedicmaterialism

~

as the deconstructionist "writes" the deconstruction

~

- the woods
publish
the poet / as the

crow e-
production

of the
settled

of the brand / all

is
- disclosed

~

- so the poet does deconstruct the "writing" - what of it? #comedicmaterialism the thyrsus statement

is

~

the thysus statement

births
generates
dendrofactifies
#comedicmaterialism

~

is

interest

the metaprice

a of collective -eproduct

in the game

of garrison/biome fluctuation? #comedicmaterialism

~

the thyrsus statement

~

#comedicmaterialism - the cunning of pure spirit

in the game

of cards, the ideal, the tale

as the device of the trace

of the biome - so the

discursive autobiograph of infinite
e-production

in the game #comedicmaterialism

~

u-topophilic e-improv #comedic #materialism

botanical e-production

in the swantological superposition

despychofetishization of psychoghettoization of the sphizopathological siphylostophistry of everyday people ~

the faculty which by means of its representations is the cause of the actuality of the objects of those representations
the intention of the ideal towards the illeity, the real (the poet

~

so the social reality is the "very" interest
that the sarcasmic thyrsus does swizzle

of the poet's #comedicmaterialism - what of it

(our poetry

in the biome

as e-producers of a

feng shui

of tree-being
as becoming-real #comedicmaterialists? #comedicmaterialism

as if #comedicmaterialism

is the production of reality ,

so desire is if

as

despite

- in the game

~

of #comedicmaterialism

it?

~

can be said, not knowing zeugs
but recreational-ly

e-producing the real

c'est moi

~

as the e-values

as number

dendrofactified

e-produce

~

- the chillness [chillheit]
of the swantologist

- a disposition to-wards [zu-wardsness-heit] a #comedicmaterialist superposition rule

of balance
of dissensus

of the clouds ~ to factify
the worlds

of their poverty - always-already-in
lake-tidally

relation
to-wards

the hungry (the wazungu) ~ [+/$]

- because in lake|tide
do not compromise our own

your hunger
to-wards / the real hungry

in the game #comedicmaterialism

~

the laws/mari-juana, the chora (Kristeva)

[/=i]

i/oeuils
i/langues
i/lands

~

- so cold
heat/pain
proprioception (the ability to know
the limbs' position

in the game/biome of #comedicmaterial metapoesis

~

- the thyrsus statement

- as the vortograph: the dionysiac
mimetic laketidal desire / in the round

superpositional

relation to the "writing-being"
discursive

to-wards

~

the stars
our zeug

#comedicmaterial
current

playas in the game
of lake

tidal
#comedic

"e-facticity" (feuerbach)

~

as the round
table

periodic
of elemental

#comedicmaterial

- infinitely displaced
in the "game

geographical paper-trace of the stage of immanence
table

- so the fucking establishment"

~

is under
stood

william
carlos
williamsically

by the sexual curves of the
fascination

of what's difficult, - so

The Bawdy Electric #comedicmaterialism

is

~

as marijuana does cause physically
laughter

that laketidal echoe of those current
playas

in the chemical human body. so,

mao #comedicmaterialism
on practice #comedicmaterialism

"All genuine knowledge has its originity in direct experience" "on practice" (july 1937) selected works, vol 1, pp. 299-300 #comedicmaterialism

~

in

the fluctuation of #comedicmaterialism

so the animals of my brain

aroused are switched / lashed
in the discursive tidefoam
of momentum eaten ethically

into facticity #comedicmaterialism

(let us get 'pataphysical) #comedicmaterialism

~

tagging the animndlfish #comedicmaterialism
in the information data sphere of the brahmin-illeity origami-trace of the lyric

curve
of the thyrsus laketemporally dendrofactifying

~

TORONTOLOGICAL DENDROFACTIFICATION IS LAKETIDAL #comedicmaterialism

~

as trees
in it

~

the kosmos infinit
if quantized tidal foam ~ so the garrison mentality does price - understand

qu'est-ce que la biome?

~

as the rhyme, #comedicmaterialism.

position/laketide

~

as pure
real

impossible
quantum

flux

as lyric
value

does the animal
neurotransmitters

a laketidal population
broadcast

- animal
domesticity

of the chemical
in our phono-textually full

probable
e-product

~

- so the schizoanalysis of the planet of noah
cognitive

of the cognate
of the trace

of the less formless formlessness of the formless curve of #comedicmaterialism

full tidally
in the round

onliness
of the choral

desiring
-biome of

early
#comedicmaterialism

~

in the age of botanical e-facticity
i.e.

in the biome. #comedicmaterialism

as Feff Melanads resigns from the centre

is a centre in time
the curve

'fro-wards
in the biome. in

~

our animal
domesticity. so the public house

is hip

to the originity
of the poet

on the side.) qu'est-ce que le biome? #comedicmaterialism

~

ix

one cannot but wonder whom

~

x

this is the game
fluxion / of the field

trip / of our spiritual #comedy

~

so - as
4/20

dawns

fingers - two fingers
rose

in co-rectitude

as the field theory is
so refined - so

the memories
is licked|

timed

who endures|in
this lyric

of the wild

bests

~

- so

the poet does call back to earlier moments

in the social atmosphere of collective desiring-production - as The Beatles

has remarked, so let it be. #comedicmaterialism

~

~

as the poet takes power

to substance ontology

oppose

laketide swantology

———

controlled substance ontology

~

to controlled substance ontology

oppose

laketide swantology

———

controlled controlled substance ontology

~

to controlled controlled substance ontology

oppose

laketide swantology

———

#comedicmaterialism

~

the position
is

in the mouth of
style

ego/ergo
torontreal/the real

~

as the wavicle / so-towards as-produced wave positions
reposed

the impossible wavicle-determination / to the supposed real

identity of indiscernible

minorities

in the game. #comedicmaterialism

~

as the tale to the lyre, so the zeug to the facticity; so
the wavicle / to the alternately possible (suppose $) (in/tide) moments of wave

-deternububg

-determining videographic mathemes

~

of antiquity #chillheit

~

is the thyrsus

a manifest

originity

of the real

de-construi?

~

INT. PATTERN POETRY -- DAY

~

Friday November 16
NIGHT

~

EXT. SPACETIDE

~

e = c = time = infinity = wave = beyond the zero = the real = impossible worlds = figlfflgiflgfligfigfligflgiflgilfglfigiflgiflgiflgfglgflgifliggl

#comedicmaterialism

~

[race/tide]

[e-production]

~

as a recreational call-back
- superpositional
the thyrsus statement
is a speech coin
?

#comedicmaterialism

~

metapoetic
- elastically numbering the superwomen in our hyperphonosphere-posterities

as the swantologist knows originity, as the #comedicmaterialist

~

- as phonemes, as ideologemes, geo
-metrically -u-topophilically discursive - as real #materials

as my love
- so

the communist society,
so wage equity. #comedicmaterialism

~

- so the standard
tidal

number
is the factified

as the wobble

~

so
desire

eats
indiscernables

in

~

am to god. #comedicmaterialism

~

as the cold, slow, wax / of the
light

undoes

the

in

~

faith, a fluctuation of our discursive impression
full

tidally
upon the tracing paper

as the swan ~ what of it?

- it goes

~

- so the snow
white

is the true
depth without

~

v.o./laketide

let

light

to be

~

wages

so the
evening

as

~

it

(th ereal

public houses

~

so -

cosmic
laketid/radiation

~

so the
holds

sets
in

our "very"
shelves

"to night" #comedicmaterialism

~

radio cool

planetary/of the sol

the real

~

i
am
field/the band

light

~

as the
e-media
of tide

as the constant

~

holds
wobble

the radio cool/flow

~

- can the de-construi . . .

so the #material

as the

momentum

d'esprit / can no be

de-termine

- is / in

-finitely ob
-tuse - so

be it. #comedicmaterialism

~

the Tag
discerning / tastefully
measure

for measure / the

Δthyrsus/laketide

does disclose / as i

factify / the public
housing - ours

on the infos
holds

e-design

as the real / brahmin-illeity

of tidal

interpellation #comedicmaterialism

as the media

the

[illegible[

~

the real
of time

"so the thyrsus
interest
in the media

unfastens updo's
into free-

-ly lawfully let
down

and hanging around
facticity, shoulders

of the libraries of reference. -- <u>Sex Panic</u>

34324828R00040

Made in the USA
San Bernardino, CA
25 May 2016